Social
Security
in
Yugoslavia

Social Security in Yugoslavia

Svetozar Pejovich

American Enterprise Institute for Public Policy Research
Washington, D.C.

Svetozar Pejovich is Dean of the Graduate School of Management at the University of Dallas, Irving, Texas, and visiting professor of economics at Texas A&M University.

I am grateful to Colin Campbell for numerous contributions to the manuscript. His intellectual drive and academic standards have made completion of the manuscript possible. Donna Malone, administrative assistant at the Graduate School of Management, has provided excellent editorial and clerical services.

Library of Congress Cataloging in Publication Data

Pejovich, Svetozar.
    Social security in Yugoslavia.

    (AEI studies ; 245)
    Bibliography: p.
    1. Social security—Yugoslavia.   I. Title.
II. Series: American Enterprise Institute for Public
Policy Research.   AEI studies ; 245.
HD7211.6.P37   368.4'009497   79-23162
ISBN 0-8447-3348-2

*HD
7211.6
.P37
1979*

AEI Studies 245

Printed in the United States of America

CONTENTS

LIST OF TABLES

INTRODUCTION

The social security system in the United States has two sides: for the beneficiaries, it is their principal source of income, and for millions who work, it is their greatest tax burden. Numerous questions have recently been raised about the system. How is it administered? What are the costs and benefits of the system? What is the effect of social security programs on income distribution, work incentives, capital formation, and the rate of innovation? This study is predicated on the assumption that comparative studies of social security in various countries will add to our understanding of the social security system in the United States.

A study of social security programs in Yugoslavia is warranted on several grounds. Yugoslavia is the first socialist state to decentralize its economy and abolish the system of administrative planning. The Yugoslav experience with economic decentralization offers a great deal of information about the advantages and limitations of the so-called market socialism. Most significantly, the Yugoslav social security system is as unusual as is that country's economic system.

Some distinctive features of the Yugoslav social security system are:

- It is organized, administered, and financed regionally.
- Within the framework of the law, the benefits and costs of the social security programs are based on a contract between those insured and the insurers.
- A major source of financing the programs is a social security tax on the wage fund. However, the wage fund in Yugoslavia is different from total wages in the United States.

The study begins with a brief outline of the Yugoslav economic system and then describes the organization of the different types of social security programs, the benefits provided, and the method of financing the programs.

1

The Yugoslav Economic System

The organization of the social security system, its programs, and its financing are consistent with and an integral part of the Yugoslav economic system. To understand the social security system in Yugoslavia, it is necessary to understand the nature of the country's economic system.

The Yugoslav government has sought to resolve economic and social problems through changes in institutional arrangements. These changes have been neither unilinear nor irreversible. The development of the Yugoslav system has proceeded slowly, reluctantly, and cyclically, and covers a thirty-year period in which, by trial and error, a unique set of institutional arrangements has been hammered out. To describe the Yugoslav economic system today as a mixture of capitalist and socialist institutions is wrong. Yugoslavia is a socialist state and its economic system is a socialist economic system. However, the government has responded uniquely—for a socialist state—to social and economic problems and proceeded to search for a set of institutional arrangements that would direct production efficiently in an environment in which capital goods cannot be privately owned. The Yugoslav economic system has become an interesting example of the interdependence of legal institutions, incentive structures, and economic processes. Nonmarket forces inherent in the coercive power of the communist leadership and supported by the bureaucracy explain the slowness and unevenness of the institutional restructuring that has occurred.

Historical Development

The Yugoslav economy has undergone four periods of substantive institutional restructuring since 1945.

In the period of administrative planning, which lasted from 1945 to 1952, the organization of the economy was similar to that of the Soviet system. Administrative planning did not work well, and the economy retrogressed. A prominent Yugoslav economist described the character of economic life in this period:

> The balancing of supply and demand in a centrally planned economy occurs in offices where a few people, unaware of the real effects of their authoritarian plans, become the supreme judges of the destinies of all producers and consumers through their bureaucratic machine. From this source of authority, plans lead further down to smaller averages according to norms born in the offices which, when they reach the enterprise level, have little resemblance to the conditions of actual life.[1]

During the period of partial decentralization from 1953 to 1964 the basic objective of the government was to create a workable economic system subject to the following general features: social ownership of nonhuman productive assets, organization of production in accordance with an overall economic plan, the right of self-management for firms and other economic units, and relaxation of direct administrative controls over business firms. During this period there was a respectable annual rate of growth of about 8 percent, high rates of inflation and unemployment (in a socialist state!), considerable misallocation of resources (the Yugoslav jargon is "political factories"), and a huge deficit in the balance of international payments.

The third period was characterized by full decentralization from 1965 to 1972. In 1965 the Yugoslav government adopted a new approach known as the "Resolution on the Basic Guidelines for Further Development of the Economic System." This resolution and the subsequent clarifying legal acts have since been referred to as the 1965 Reform. Its basic objective was to create an institutional environment that would promote economic efficiency by encouraging individual initiative. Some of its key features were:

- The system of administrative planning shifted from annual operational plans to long-range development plans, which are no more than a hazy vision of things that would be nice to have. Administrative planning came to an end in Yugoslavia in the late 1960s.

---

[1] Quoted from A. Waterston, *Planning in Yugoslavia* (Washington, D. C.: World Bank, 1962), p. 19. The statement is attributed to late professor R. Bicanich from the University of Zagreb.

- The government transferred to the banking system the responsibility for controlling both the pattern and the rate of debt financing. The relation between firms and banks was fully commercialized in the late 1960s.
- A major objective of the 1965 Reform was to promote economic efficiency by changing the system of incentives. The Yugoslav government granted the labor-managed firm greater independence from administrative controls, promised to enlarge the share of the net product left to the firm from 50 percent in 1964 to 70 percent in 1971 (this promise was not fulfilled), and allowed the firm to determine freely the allocation of its income among its wage fund, additions to the capital assets (self-financed investment), and other internal funds. Since the rate of interest on individual savings was about 6 percent in 1965, while the average marginal productivity of capital was estimated at almost 30 percent,[2] Yugoslav economists as well as government decision makers expected that workers would in their self-interest seek higher future incomes by reinvesting the firm's earnings.[3]

The expected results of the 1965 Reform never materialized. The government failed to foresee the behavioral effects of prevailing property relations on the allocation of firms' earnings.[4] The failure to appreciate properly the relationships among the property rights structure, the penalty-reward systems, and economic behavior became obvious by 1970. The percentage of earnings allocated to the wage fund rose from 69 percent in 1964 to over 80 percent in 1970; the percentage of the firm's capital investment financed by the banking system rose from 9 percent in 1963 to over 50 percent in 1971; the cost of living doubled during the 1965–1971 period; firms found their transactions balances seriously depleted; and the rate of unemployment approached 10 percent of the labor force *exclusive* of about 1 million Yugoslavs who left the country to seek work in the capitalist West. The structure of property rights established by the 1965 Reform

[2] D. Vojnic, *Investicije i Fiksni Fondovi Yugoslavije* (Zagreb: Ekonomski Institut, 1973), p. 73.

[3] The employees of the Yugoslav firm have two major wealth-increasing alternatives: joint investment in earning assets of the firm via retained earnings (unowned assets), and individual investment in other assets (owned assets). Joint investment does not allow for withdrawal of invested capital. A worker loses all his claims to future returns from the firm's assets once he quits the job.

[4] For a behavioral analysis of the Yugoslav firm, see E. Furubotn and S. Pejovich, "Property Rights, Economic Decentralization and the Evolution of the Yugoslav Firm 1965–1972," *Journal of Law and Economics*, vol. 16 (October 1973), pp. 275–302.

generated behavior that was disappointing. The government then responded by embarking on yet another round of institutional restructuring.

The fourth period, one of contractual self-management, began in the early 1970s and is described in the 1974 Constitution.[5] The main characteristics of this system are: the principle of self-management, the sharing of property rights by government and by workers using the property, and a system of contracts among self-managing units.

The Principle of Self-Management

Article 1 of the 1974 Constitution states that "the Socialist Federal Republic of Yugoslavia is a federal state . . . based on the power of and self-management by the working class and all working people." Article 10 defines the Yugoslav social and economic system as being "based on freely associated labor and socially owned means of production, and on self-management by the working people in production and in the distribution of the social product in basic and other organizations of associated labor." "Social product" corresponds to the gross national product (GNP), and "organizations of associated labor" is a Yugoslav legal expression for economic as well as noneconomic activities (cultural, educational, and social) performed by workers with socially owned assets and organized on the principles of self-management.

The social and economic basis of self-management in Yugoslavia lies in the state's right of ownership of capital goods; the employees' right of ownership of the returns from capital goods; the employees' right to approve, police, and enforce the decisions made by the managers of their institutions; and the system of contracts among self-managing organizations. In a capitalist country, allocative decisions are made by owners either directly or through hired managers. In a centrally planned socialist state, allocative decisions are made by the ruling elite through either the party apparatus or the state bureaucracy. In Yugoslavia, allocative decisions are allegedly made by those who work with capital assets (associated labor). This is the trademark of the principle of self-management in Yugoslavia.

---

[5] It is clear that the ruling elite interferes with the economic decision-making processes in self-managing units, but this point should not be exaggerated. Behavior generated by the prevailing property rights tends to dampen the party's influence, and as orders and instructions travel down from the top they are modified and adjusted to suit local conditions. Party members employed by self-managing units have frequently faced the problem of their loyalty to the party on the one hand and self-interest within their economic units on the other.

The Law of Associated Labor of 1976 translated the constitutional principle of self-management into a set of explicit rules and guidelines. It is a major operational document that sets forth the concept of self-management as understood, interpreted, and implemented in Yugoslavia.

Decision-Making Units

The term "firm" has been completely eliminated from Yugoslav legal jargon. More than the mere substitution of one term for another, there was a major change in the organization of team production processes in the early 1970s. Yugoslav law makes an important distinction between the "organization of associated labor" and "the basic organization of associated labor." These terms are cumbersome and so similar that this study will use the terms "parent organization" and "member organization" respectively. Both terms are all-embracing. They include all commercial establishments, institutions, and other organizations in which human labor is combined with capital assets. The right of an organization to be a self-managing unit depends on this association of live labor and capital.

Parent organizations include all economic as well as noneconomic organizations that are self-managed and carry out their activities using socially owned capital goods. The parent organization "is in fact what was earlier referred to as an enterprise in the economic sector and an institution in the noneconomic sector."[6] It may include one or more members, smaller operating organizations of associated labor that are independent but component parts of the parent organization. Member organizations correspond to plants or departments and are the fundamental economic units in the Yugoslav economic system. The law states that if the results of their joint labor can be measured in terms of value either in the market or within the parent organization, and can be independently expressed, the employees should form their own member organization. The identifiability and separability of the flow of receipts are the major factors in determining whether the unit should be independent. Most significantly, according to the law, a member organization has the right to leave its parent organization provided that the benefits it is expected to receive from leaving exceed the cost borne by other member organizations that remain in it.

---

[6] *The Constitution of the Socialist Federal Republic of Yugoslavia* (Belgrade, 1974), p. 307.

Moreover, the member organization must compensate those who remain with the parent organization.[7]

Employee Control. The right to govern a member organization is vested in all of its employees, while the right to operate it is granted to the director (*poslovodni organ*). The employees exercise their right of governing the member organization both directly and indirectly.

The forms of direct control are general meetings and referendums. Indirectly, employees govern through the Workers' Council, the highest organ of management in the member organization. Delegates are elected to the Workers' Council by the employees for a two-year term. In order to prevent the development of a closed governing group, they can be reelected only once.

The manager of a member organization is the chief executive officer. He is appointed (and fired) by the Workers' Council, which must advertise the position in the media and select the manager from among the qualified applicants. The manager is responsible for the development, search, and formulation of long-run and short-run policies. He identifies investment alternatives and proposes business strategies. The Workers' Council makes the final choices from among the alternatives presented by the manager. The manager's evaluation and his method of presentation of the available alternatives necessarily influence the choices of the Workers' Council.

A parent organization has its own Workers' Council composed of representatives of the member organizations. The council elects the director of the parent organization, who must cooperate with managers of the member organizations. The relationships among member organizations and their rights, obligations, and responsibilities with respect to the parent organization are regulated by contractual agreements.

Joint Organizations. Yugoslavia has its own conglomerates. Parent organizations may join together in a joint organization of associated labor. The Workers' Council of such an organization consists of delegates nominated by parent organizations. This Workers' Council elects the director who, in turn, must cooperate with directors of member enterprises. The relationships among parent organizations in the joint organization are also regulated by contractual agreements.

---

[7] *Nacrt Zakona o Udruzenom Radu* [Draft of the Law of Associated Labor] (Belgrade, 1976), pp. 111–12.

Property Rights

Most capital goods used in productive enterprises cannot be privately owned. Individual investment in Yugoslavia is restricted to savings accounts, jewelry, human capital, and a few types of physical assets such as small shops, small farms, homes, second homes, small rooming houses, restaurants, and taxis, where private property rights do not necessarily and obviously violate the principle of social (state) ownership.

The government had to reconcile the constitutional principle of self-management with the constitutional requirement of state ownership of capital goods. That was accomplished through a series of changes in property rights starting with the law on the Management of Commercial Enterprises by Workers' Collectives (June 1950) and the law on the Management of Fixed Capital Goods of Enterprises (December 1953). Basically, property rights in Yugoslavia are shared: the state owns most capital goods, but employees have a right to the earnings of their respective economic units, which are partly the result of capital inputs.

Member organizations do not own the capital goods in their possession. Each must maintain the book value of its assets by taking into account depreciation and by remitting the proceeds from the sale of capital goods. The state's ownership of capital goods held by the basic organization is affirmed by this requirement. The state, however, cannot take capital goods away from working collectives, and the member organizations are free to decide how to use the capital goods in their possession. A member organization is free to change the composition of its assets, for example, to substitute one type of asset (cash) for another (machines). It can rent assets, sell them to other organizations, or produce them for its own use. If an asset is sold for less than its book value, the difference has to be made up from the organization's earnings by buying capital goods in the market.

The employees of a member organization have the right to the organization's net income. Employee participation in the distribution of earnings has replaced a system of wages and is the essential feature of self-management in Yugoslavia. Factors that affect the formation and distribution of net income (legal norms and constitutional constraints) significantly influence the behavior of member organizations.[8]

[8] For a detailed analysis, see E. Furubotn and S. Pejovich, "The Formation and Distribution of Net Product and the Behavior of the Yugoslav Firm," *Jahrbuch der Wirtschaft Osteuropas*, vol. 3 (Munich: Veröffentlichung des Osteuropa Institut, 1972), pp. 265–88.

These factors link the system of rewards and productivity responses in the Yugoslav economy.

Sources of Income for Workers

Yugoslav law recognizes three major sources of total revenue for a member organization: the sale of goods and services, the value of internal transactions, and the returns on external investments. The term "internal transactions" refers to the value of transactions between member organizations within the parent organization (for example, services of the shipping department in a manufacturing enterprise). Those transactions are valued at prevailing market prices. External investments consist of time deposits, credits to other self-managing organizations, and joint projects undertaken by two or more member organizations.

The uses of the total revenue of member organizations are divided into three categories: expenditures, amortization, and net product. Expenditures include the cost of all inputs. In addition, turnover taxes on the sale of final goods, as well as customs duties, are included in such expenses. Turnover taxes vary from one product to another, and from one region to another. Although the law requires minimum depreciation rates, a collective may depreciate assets at a higher rate if it wishes. An asset that has been fully depreciated, but is still productive, must be reappraised at its market price. If a fully depreciated asset is sold to another organization, the proceeds must be allocated to what is known as the business fund.

The net income, or *dohodak*, is the amount of the organization's total revenue to be paid out. The residual includes the returns to labor after legal and contractual obligations are paid. There are numerous legal obligations plus obligatory contributions to less developed areas that must be met from dohodak. (Among them are the general tax, the social consumption tax, the contribution for national defense, and insurance premiums.) The residual belongs to the member organization and is divided among four funds—the wage fund, the collective consumption fund, the business fund, and the reserve fund. The allocation of the residual among the four funds is up to the organization. In the first quarter of 1978, the share of dohodak going to the four funds totaled 63 percent; that is, legal and contractual obligations amounted to 37 percent.

The allocation to the business fund together with depreciation allowances provides funds for new investment. From the point of view of the employees, every dollar of the residual that is allocated to the business fund reduces their current incomes but, at the same time, promises larger incomes in the future. The purpose of the reserve fund is to cover losses, protect the organization against emergencies, and make payments to employees when their incomes fall below the legal minimum. The purpose of the collective consumption fund is to improve the general standard of living of the employees, and it includes subsidies for apartments, child care centers, recreation halls, scholarships, and resort homes.

The wage fund is subject to various taxes, including the social security tax. Those taxes amount to about 31 percent of the wage fund (or about 19 percent of dohodak). The rules for the distribution of the after-tax wage fund among the employees are determined by the organization. These rules must be clearly defined and announced in advance by the Workers' Council. In most organizations, the distribution of the wage fund is determined by attaching a specified number of points to each job in the organization. While the criteria for determining the number of points for each position differ among organizations, the following factors are frequently stressed: required skills, education, health risks, and hardships. The wage fund is then divided by the total number of points in the organization. That procedure determines the value of a point per accounting period. Next, the value of a point is multiplied by the number of points associated with each job to arrive at the employee's income for that period.

The System of Contracts

The Yugoslav economy today rests on a system of contractual agreements within as well as among decision-making units. Since this feature of the economy is crucial for an understanding of the social security system in Yugoslavia, some important contractual arrangements are described here.

The employees in a member organization make decisions, either directly or through elected representatives, that have important economic consequences for the future. They also capture the future benefits and bear the cost of these decisions. Within the set of legal constraints, employees are equal contractual partners in the team decision-making processes.

Member organizations that belong to the same parent organization negotiate a contract with each other that specifies their rights and obligations. This must be made public. Within limits, the terms of contractual agreements vary from one institution to another. In general, these agreements specify the composition of decision-making bodies, take into account the production and financial plans of organizations, assign costs of law suits and other damages (usually to the parent organization although these costs are shifted internally to the member organizations responsible for them), and regulate commercial relations between member organizations. Given the structure of property rights, independent units in a parent organization have strong incentives to negotiate contractual terms that are consistent with prevailing market conditions.

Self-management agreements regulate issues of common interest to workers in the organization, the employees in local communities, and other self-managing organizations in related activities. Those agreements provide for the pooling of resources in joint undertakings, cover the division of labor, establish criteria for the distribution of income within the participating organizations, and address other questions concerning their cooperation. The important function of self-management agreements is to replace the regulative role of the state with respect to the relations among the participating organizations.

Social contracts are negotiated by groups bound together by broad common interests—production units, trade unions, trade associations, sociopolitical organizations, and government agencies. Social contracts are supposed to regulate questions of common interest and replace the state in the resolution of key economic issues.

Finally, the provision of many services such as welfare, health, education, and power production is negotiated contractually between (1) economic organizations, other institutions, and citizens' groups and (2) those who supply those services. Such contractual associations cover a region or locality. Those are called self-managing communities of interest. Self-managing communities of interest in the fields of health and retirement administer the social security programs.

The economic system of Yugoslavia is based on contractual agreements made in a prescribed form. These agreements encompass the entire social and economic life of the country. Within certain constraints, the terms of contracts are negotiated among the participants. Since contractual agreements are mandated by law and the basic constraints are frequently stipulated in advance, the agreements are not entirely voluntary. A consequence of the system is that the role of the state in regulating and controlling economic life is reduced. The system of self-management generates incentives for those entering into contracts to seek a reduction in the prevailing legal contraints and, consequently, to obtain greater freedom in negotiating the terms of agreements.

10

2
The Social Security System's Organizational Structure

The Yugoslav social security system consists of two major programs: (1) retirement, survivors', and disability payments, and (2) health services. Although the organizations administering the two programs are independent of each other, both programs are organized in much the same way.

Contractual Aspects

The Yugoslav social security system adheres to the principle of self-management rather than being administered by a state agency. Social security taxes are not paid into a state budget, and benefits are not provided through state budgets. Article 53 of the 1974 Constitution states:

> In order to ensure social security working people shall form self-managing communities of interest . . . in which they will pool resources for the purpose and determine . . . their common and individual obligations toward those communities and the common and individual rights they will realize in them.

A self-managing community of interest is a contractual entity created by organizations representing those who supply certain services and organizations representing those who demand them. Specifically, Yugoslav law mandates that self-managing communities of interest be formed to provide education, scientific research, cultural needs, health services, and social welfare.

To provide retirement and disability benefits, self-management agreements cover those who are insured as well as those who are already receiving benefits. To provide health services, self-management agreements are made between representatives of those who are eligible (by law) to receive such services and self-managing organizations which perform those services, such as hospitals, clinics, medical institutes, ambulances, and pharmacies.

Regional Setup

Basic self-managing communities of interest (one in the field of health and another in the field of retirement and disability) are organized in each local area. Over these local groups is a regional self-managing community of interest. Territorial boundaries of the regions are determined by such factors as the economic conditions of life in the area, the homogeneity of the population, the availability of health services, and the number of retired and disabled persons. These regional self-managing communities of interest administer the social security programs in the six republics and two autonomous provinces.

The self-management agreement specifies the territory to be included, the method of financing the programs, the method of choosing the governing bodies, and the procedure for resolving conflicts among the participants. In the field of health, the agreement must also specify the relationship between those insured and the insurers, while in the field of retirement and disability, the agreement must establish the relationship between those insured and those already receiving benefits. Since taxes are set by regions for health care programs, and by the republics for retirement and disability programs, tax rates vary.

Yugoslav law requires that there be only one self-managing community of interest for each region for health programs and one for retirement and disability programs. The law also requires that a contractual agreement be arrived at. If the participants fail to agree on the terms of the contract, the appropriate government (local, regional, or republic) may step in and resolve the dispute. Article 125 of the 1974 Constitution states:

> The assemblies of the [relevant government] shall stimulate the conclusion of self-management agreement and social contracts and may make it obligatory for specific self-managing organizations and communities to conduct proceedings for the conclusions of self-management agreements or social contracts.

The law distinguishes between the right to govern a self-managing community of interest and the right to operate it. The right to govern is vested in all the members affected, while the operation is entrusted to agencies (*sluzba*) established to administer those programs.

The Assembly and Executive Board

Members of a self-managing community of interest exercise their right of self-government in two ways: directly and indirectly through elected representatives. The direct controls include general meetings and referendums. General meetings may be called by the official assembly representing the self-managing community of interest or by a group of individuals. The purpose of general meetings is to discuss critical issues and problems that have to be resolved. Referendums are held to adopt substantive changes in the self-management agreement. The vote is secret and the majority decision is binding.

Members govern their self-managing community of interest indirectly through an assembly and an executive board. Member organizations are represented in the assembly by elected delegates in proportion to their size. Delegates can be reelected only once.

The assembly is the highest organ of government in a self-managing community of interest. In the field of retirement and disability, the insured and those receiving benefits elect delegates in proportion to their numbers. In the field of health, the assembly has two councils representing the insured and the insurers; however, the small Republic of Montenegro has only one regional health organization. Decisions on taxes, approved drugs, and acceptable standards of health care must be approved by a majority vote in each council of the assembly.

Although delegates to the assembly continue to work at their regular jobs and receive no additional salary, they are reimbursed for expenses incurred in the performance of their duties. The assembly enacts the by-laws of the group, specifies the services to be provided, and makes plans for new or expanded programs. The assembly determines the taxes that members of the self-managing community of interest must pay, elects the executive board from among its own members, and approves contractual agreements with other institutions.

The executive board prepares financial plans, controls revenues and expenditures, keeps abreast of new laws and regulations on matters of importance in the field, and appoints and supervises the administrative staff of member groups. As in the assembly, the executive board makes decisions by majority vote.

Administration

A self-managing community of interest forms its own administrative agency, or sluzba. The regional assembly, in consultation with the appropriate government, appoints the director, the chief executive officer, who is appointed for a specific period of time (usually four years) and can be reappointed any number of times. The assembly can fire the director before the end of his term in office if he refuses to execute the decisions of the assembly, violates the regulations of the self-managing community of interest, incurs major financial losses, or prevents members of the group from exercising their rights of self-management.

The administrators of a self-managing community of interest execute the decisions of the assembly and executive board, take care of administrative, technical, and financial affairs, prepare statistical tables, and perform all other tasks delegated to them by the organization.

The sluzba is itself a self-managing entity. It negotiates an agreement with the larger group it services. The agreement specifies its rights, obligations, and responsibilities as well as its budget. The administrators run their internal affairs, including hiring, wage determination, and other management policies, in much the same way as in other economic organizations.

The Role of the State

Self-management agreements have replaced the direct involvement of the state in health and retirement programs. These agreements provide for smaller bureaucratic units (sluzba) that are less costly to monitor than centralized administrations. Yet the Yugoslav government has preserved for itself the final authority to judge the content of self-management agreements. It may be necessary for the government to intervene when contractual partners fail to arrive at self-management agreements that are mandated by the law, or when they conclude agreements that violate legal constraints. In addition, the government has also reserved for itself the right to rescind unilaterally a self-management agreement whenever the government determines that it is socially "harmful." Article 130 of the Yugoslav Constitution is explicit on this point:

> If in an organization of associated labor or another self-managing organization or community self-management relations have become essentially disrupted, or if serious harm has been caused to social interests . . . the assembly of [the appropriate government] shall have the right . . . to dissolve the workers' council or another corresponding managing body . . . and to call for new elections for the members of this body . . . temporarily to restrict the realization of certain self-management rights of the working people and managing bodies, and to take other measures as spelled out by statute.

3
Retirement, Disability, and Survivors' Benefits

In Yugoslavia eligibility for benefits is based on a person's employment or personal characteristics. This is different from the social security system in the United States, in which persons have to pay taxes for a certain number of quarters in order to be eligible. In the United States the social security system was initially proposed as an insurance system, and the eligibility requirements still reflect the conception of an insurance program in which employers and employees are purchasing an annuity. Actually, the system developed into a pay-as-you-go program, and there is currently only a very loose relationship between the amount of taxes paid in and the benefits a person receives.

In Yugoslavia, the persons who are by law eligible to receive retirement and disability benefits include:

Full-time employees in self-managing organizations, communities, sociopolitical organizations, and private firms
Part-time employees who work at least half the regular working time
Full-time members of artisans and fishing cooperatives
Disabled workers and war veterans
Self-employed persons (for example, attorneys).

In addition, the following are eligible to receive disability benefits:

Soldiers
Unemployed persons, provided they are registered and actively seeking work
Retirees
Voluntary workers at projects of social significance.

The following persons also are eligible to receive disability benefits, provided that disability was caused by the nature of their work:

Trainees in vocational and technical schools

High school and university students

Part-time employees who work less than half the regular working time.

In Yugoslavia those not eligible for retirement and disability benefits are primarily the unemployed not actively seeking work.

Retirement Benefits

In Yugoslavia the date of eligibility for a retirement pension depends on age or years of service, or both. This is different from the social security system in the United States, in which persons are not entitled to a retirement benefit before age sixty-two (sixty for widows) regardless of years of service. A Yugoslav becomes eligible to receive a retirement pension under one of the following conditions:

- Forty years of service for men and thirty-five years of service for women. If a person fulfills one of these amounts of service, there is no age requirement.
- Sixty-five years of age for men and sixty years of age for women if a person has at least fifteen years of service, provided that the person has worked forty months in the last five years or eighty months in the last ten years.
- Sixty years of age for men and fifty-five years of age for women if they have at least twenty years of service.
- Early retirement at fifty-five years of age for men with at least thirty-five years of service and at fifty years of age for women with at least thirty years of service. However, the amount of the pension is reduced by 1.33 percent for each year of early retirement. (For example, the amount of the pension would be reduced by 6.65 percent if a man retired at age fifty-five with thirty-five years of service.)

In Yugoslavia the differences in the eligibility requirements for men and women have not been removed. In recent years, differences in the treatment of men and women in the social security system in the United States have been greatly reduced. In the United States, for example, women became eligible in 1956 for retirement benefits at age sixty-two. This same provision was extended to men in 1961. In Yugoslavia there are no benefits for spouses of eligible workers as there are in the United States.

In general, a person in Yugoslavia cannot work and still receive a retirement benefit. In the United States, the work income test required for eligibility for a retirement benefit is complicated. Persons between ages sixty-two and seventy-two who earn more than a certain amount have had their benefits reduced $1 for every additional $2 earned, up until the benefit is completely exhausted. The system in the United States permits retired persons to receive limited earnings (usually from part-time employment) without losing benefits.

The monthly pension received by a retiree in Yugoslavia depends, initially, on his years of service, his earnings base, and the adjustment allowed for inflation. After retirement, his monthly pension depends on the adjustments made for inflation and the real rate of economic growth.

Years of Service. A Yugoslav begins to count his years of service from the age of fifteen, and all calendar years during which he was employed on a full-time basis are counted. In addition, the Yugoslav social security programs grant full years of service credit to unemployed persons who are registered and actively looking for work (for up to two years), to Yugoslavs who are employed by international organizations or foreign firms, and to persons sent to scientific institutes to improve their skills and education.

Part-time work is adjusted to its full-time equivalent and then added to one's years of service. Suppose that Marko worked five hours a day during 1978, but in that same year full-time employees at his place of employment worked eight hours per day. The full-time equivalent of Marko's part-time work is then:

$$\frac{365 \text{ calendar days} \times 5 \text{ hours}}{8 \text{ hours}} = 7.5 \text{ months}$$

Part-time work is sometimes counted as full-time work in the case of disabled workers and war veterans who cannot work full-time, mothers with infant children, people going through rehabilitation programs, and some others.

An unusual feature of the Yugoslav system is that the law gives employees in jobs that are relatively difficult or likely to cause health hazards more than one year of service credit for each year of full-time employment. The maximum extra credit is 50 percent. For example, one year of employment in coal mines adds eighteen months to one's years of service; one year of work in steel mills gives the worker fifteen months' credit for each year of full-time work; and fire fighters get fifteen months' credit for each year of employment.

In addition, some people receive years of service credit for special services of national interest. For example, Yugoslav citizens who participated in illegal revolutionary work before April 1941 (just before World War II) receive full credit, participants in civil war (on Tito's side) get two years of service credit for each year in the woods, and prisoners of war get full credit for years spent in war camps.

Table 1 shows that the amount of the retirement benefit received by a worker in Yugoslavia varies with his or her years of service.

TABLE 1

Years-of-Service and Percentage of Earnings Base Used to Calculate Retirement Benefits

Years of Service	Percentage of Earnings Base	
	Men	Women
15	35	40
16	37	43
17	39	46
18	41	49
19	43	52
20	45	55
21	47	57
22	49	59
23	51	61
24	53	63
25	55	65
26	57	67
27	59	69
28	61	71
29	63	73
30	65	75
31	68	77
32	69	79
33	71	81
34	73	83
35	75	85
36	77	—
37	79	—
38	81	—
39	83	—
40	85	—

Dash (—): Not applicable.
SOURCE: *Udruzeni Rad i Osnovna Prava iz Penzijskog i Invalidskog Osiguranja* (Belgrade: Praksa, 1976), p. 13.

18

This table is for the republic of Serbia, but the system is similar to those in other regions. There is strong inducement not only for each man to work forty years before he retires, but also for each woman to work thirty-five years. In the United States wives of eligible workers are entitled to retirement benefits even though they have no employment record. This is not the case in Yugoslavia. Note also in Table 1 the significantly higher rates awarded to women than to men. Treating women differently from men is now illegal in the United States. In addition, the percentage of the earnings base used in calculating U.S. social security benefits does not vary with years of service but is instead progressive—a person with a small earnings base receives a larger pension relative to his earnings base than a person with a large earnings base. In the new benefit formula established by Congress in 1977, 90 percent is allowed of the first $180 of the average monthly earnings base, 32 percent of the next $905, and 15 percent of an average monthly earnings base above $1,085.

Earnings Base. A Yugoslav's earnings base, from which his pension is computed, equals his average monthly income in the last ten years (or any consecutive ten years of the retiree's choice). The earnings base times the appropriate percentage shown in Table 1 determines the retiree's unadjusted monthly pension. In the United States the earnings base includes all years of employment from 1951 to the year prior to that in which a person attains age sixty-two, except for the five years of lowest earnings. If a person continues to work past age sixty-two, these additional years of earnings may be substituted for earlier years of lower earnings.

In Yugoslavia, if the retiree worked either part-time or overtime during the last ten years, adjustment is made to express his earnings in full-time monthly equivalents. Those employed by private employers are subject to a special limitation that tends to reduce their pensions; annual increments in their incomes over their ten-year base period are limited to the average income increase for the region. For example, the social security system in Serbia used the limits in Table 2 for the 1966–1975 period.

Each republic also has a ceiling on the earnings base. The maximum earnings base for the 1965–1976 period in Serbia is shown in Table 3. The average net personal income in Serbia was 3,408 dinars in 1976, but since the ceiling was almost three times this amount only the highest income groups were affected. There is no minimum pension as there is in the United States and no private pension plans in Yugoslavia.

TABLE 2

LIMITATIONS ON THE ANNUAL INCREASE IN INCOMES EARNED IN THE
PRIVATE SECTOR FOR DETERMINATION OF THE EARNINGS BASE,
SERBIA, 1966–1975

Year	Maximum Percentage Increase over Preceding Year
1966	42.0
1967	14.3
1968	8.4
1969	14.7
1970	15.4
1971	20.7
1972	16.6
1973	16.4
1974	29.3
1975	23.0

NOTE: The private sector consists of small shops, restaurants, taxi businesses, small rooming houses, and handicraft stores.

SOURCE: *Prirucnik za Primenu Propisa o Penzijskom i Invalidskom Osiguranju* (Belgrade: Center za Informacije, 1976), p. 82.

TABLE 3

MAXIMUM EARNINGS BASE, SERBIA, 1965–1976

Year	Amount per Year (dinars)[a]
1965	1,550
1966	2,400
1967	2,520
1968	2,709
1969	3,000
1970	3,252
1971	3,824
1972	4,474
1973	5,235
1974	6,265
1975	8,189
1976	9,993

[a] A dollar equaled approximately eighteen dinars in 1978.

SOURCE: *Prirucnik za Primenu Propisa*, p. 81.

Because workers' pay depends on the residual earned by their self-managing organizations, there are often significant differences in incomes among the workers employed by different enterprises in the same area. A blue-collar worker in one enterprise may earn more than a white-collar worker in another and consequently will have a larger pension. Two workers with identical skills doing the same job in two different self-managing organizations may also have significantly different earnings.

Disability Benefits

Yugoslav law distinguishes among three types of disability. The first category is for disabilities that make a person totally and permanently unable to perform either his current job or a similar job commensurate with his qualifications and experience. The second category is for the permanently reduced capacity to work. The third comprises disabilities that render a person permanently unable to work at his former job, but able to work full-time at another job commensurate with his qualifications and experience.

In determining an insured's rights to receive disability benefits, the Yugoslav law distinguishes between disability caused at work as a result of an accident or work-related illness, and disability resulting from an accident or illness not suffered on the job. This distinction is not made by the U.S. social security system. The Yugoslav law interprets a disability as being work-related if it was incurred during travel to and from work, or official travel, while participating in public work of social interest, or during military exercises.

Whenever disability is work-related, disability benefits are equal to retirement benefits received by men who have forty years of service (or women who have thirty-five years of service). The insured receives 85 percent of his earnings base. If he worked less than ten years, the earnings base is the average adjusted monthly income over the years worked.

Non-work-related disability qualifies a person for benefits if his years of service include three out of every four years between the age of twenty and the time he becomes unable to work. Under certain conditions, he may also be eligible to receive benefits if his years of service include at least one-third of his working life. For disabled persons with twenty years of service, disability benefits are determined in the same manner as retirement benefits. The appropriate percentage in Table 1 would be applied to their earnings base (their average adjusted monthly income over the last ten years). However, when the insured has less than twenty years of service and his age is below sixty (fifty-five for women), disability benefits are 45 percent and 55 percent of the earnings base for men and women respectively.

Workers in the second category of disability are eligible to receive temporary disability benefits equal to 90 percent of what their regular disability benefits would be until they reach sixty years of age (fifty-five for women). At that age, they become eligible for regular disability benefits. A disabled person classified under the third category and older than forty-five (forty for women) is also entitled to a temporary pension of 90 percent of full disability benefits.

Professional Retraining and Employment. A partially disabled person in Yugoslavia is said to have the right to employment; he is also eligible for retraining if below forty-five years of age (forty years for women). When disability is not work-related, the insured is eligible for employment and retraining usually only if his years of service include two out of every three years between the age of twenty and the occurrence of partial disability. When disability is work-related, however, the right to employment and retraining does not depend on the years of service.

Self-managing groups as well as private employers must either employ or retrain their disabled employees, or find them employment or retraining at other institutions. In addition, while in retraining programs or shifting jobs, disabled persons are entitled to compensation equal to 90 percent of their former monthly incomes.

Reimbursement for Physical Injuries. An insured person is eligible to receive monthly social security payments for physical injuries specifically listed in social contracts. The amount of reimbursement depends on the causes and extent of injury.

Physical injuries are classified according to the percentage of physical injury. Table 4 shows the amount of monthly payment for the eight classes of injury stipulated by the social security law in Serbia.

Survivors' Benefits

Most dependents of deceased workers are eligible for survivors' benefits: surviving spouses; legitimate, illegitimate and adopted children; dependent grandchildren without parents; and dependent parents.

In order for dependents to receive survivors' benefits, the insured

TABLE 4

Reimbursement for Physical Injuries, Serbia

Classification of Injury	Amount of Physical Injury (percent)	Reimbursement for Injuries at Work (dinars)	Reimbursement for Injuries Elsewhere (dinars)
1	100	367	186
2	90	331	168
3	80	294	149
4	70	257	130
5	60	220	112
6	50	189	93
7	40	149	74
8	30	110	56

Source: *Prirucnik za Primenu Propisa*, p. 302.

must have been eligible for retirement or disability benefits at the time of death. A surviving wife is eligible at forty-five years of age if she is unable to work. A surviving husband is eligible for survivors' benefits if he is either sixty years old or unable to work. Children are eligible to receive survivors' benefits if they are unable to work or are under age fifteen. Children attending school may receive benefits until the age of twenty-six.

The amount of survivors' benefits depends on the insured's earnings base and the number of family members who qualify for benefits. Table 5 shows how the level of survivors' benefits is determined in Serbia.

TABLE 5

Survivors' Benefits, Serbia

Number of Family Members	Percentage of Full Retirement Benefits
1	70
2	80
3	90
4 or more	100

Source: *Prirucnik za Primenu Propisa*, pp. 111–113.

Adjustments in Benefits

Adjustments for Inflation. Adjustments for inflation are based on the rate of inflation in each region and differ from one area to another. The revised technique of adjusting benefits for inflation adopted in the United States in 1977 is similar to the technique used in Yugoslavia, although the U.S. adjustment does not vary from state to state but is the same throughout the country.

Yugoslav social security benefits for people already retired are adjusted annually for inflation. When the rate of inflation is less than 3 percent, no adjustment is made in that year. However, the rate of inflation in that year (say, 2 percent) is added to the rate of inflation in the next year (say, 5 percent) and the adjustment is made using the combined rate (7 percent). Table 6 shows the annual adjustment for inflation in Serbia from 1967 to 1975.

The second type of adjustment is for those who are about to begin receiving retirement, disability, or survivors' benefits. The earnings base of such persons is adjusted for inflation. Monthly incomes from earlier years are expressed in terms of their equivalents in the current year for each republic. The coefficients are revised each year to take account of the current rate of inflation. In the United States, for those still employed, wages in prior years are indexed to average covered wages of all workers rather than to consumer prices. In Yugoslavia there is an adjustment for real growth, which is explained

TABLE 6

ANNUAL ADJUSTMENTS IN RETIREMENT BENEFITS FOR INFLATION, SERBIA, 1967–1975

Year	Increase in Retirement Benefits
1967	7.5
1968	5.0
1969	8.4
1970	12.0
1971	17.0
1972	17.0
1973	17.0
1974	21.7
1975	23.5

SOURCE: *Prirucnik za Primenu Propisa*, pp. 292–317.

below, in addition to the adjustment for inflation. The overall adjustments in benefits in the two countries are very similar.

Table 7 shows the changes in the inflation adjustment coefficients in the earnings base in Serbia from 1964 to 1976. Table 8 shows differences in those coefficients among six republics and two autonomous provinces for individuals retiring between July 1975 and June 1976 with identical unadjusted monthly money incomes over the last ten years. The last year included in their respective earnings base is 1975. Each person's income in a given year is multiplied by the coefficient for the year and the results are added up and divided by ten (years). The result is the adjusted earnings base for each individual. Assuming that they each had forty years of service, the basic pension is multiplied by 0.85 (see Table 1) to obtain the initial monthly pension shown in Table 9. There are regional differences in benefits for individuals with identical earnings histories.

Adjustments for Real Growth. This adjustment is necessary to compensate former workers for adding to their organization's capital stock and is related to the property right structure in Yugoslavia. The basic organization of associated labor determines, through its Workers' Council, the allocation of dohodak (net income) among the

TABLE 7

ADJUSTMENT COEFFICIENTS FOR INDEXING THE EARNINGS BASE,
SERBIA, 1964–1976

Year	Coefficients in 1974	Coefficients in 1975	Coefficients in 1976
1964	5.276	6.822	8.389
1965	3.822	4.942	6.077
1966	2.702	3.501	4.306
1967	2.356	3.046	3.746
1968	2.167	2.801	3.445
1969	1.890	2.443	3.004
1970	1.638	2.117	2.604
1971	1.357	1.755	2.158
1972	1.164	1.505	1.851
1973	1.000	1.293	1.590
1974	—	1.000	1.230
1975	—	—	1.000
1976	—	—	—

SOURCE: *Udruzeni Rad i Osnovna Prava*, p. 12, and *Prirucnik za Primenu Propisa*, pp. 238–239.

TABLE 8

Adjustment Coefficients for the Earnings Base, by Republics, 1966–1975

Year	Assumed Monthly Income of Worker (dinars)	Bosnia and Hercegovina	Monte-negro	Croatia	Macedonia	Slovenia	Serbia	Kosovo	Vojvodina
1966	1,000	3.65	3.59	3.62	3.60	3.42	3.50	3.74	3.70
1967	1,200	3.28	3.13	3.16	3.10	3.09	3.05	3.25	3.28
1968	1,400	2.98	2.86	2.90	2.83	2.82	2.80	3.96	3.07
1969	1,600	2.60	2.46	2.50	2.52	2.45	2.44	2.64	2.64
1970	1,800	2.12	2.08	2.09	2.14	2.05	2.12	2.29	2.25
1971	2,000	1.74	1.73	1.68	1.79	1.71	1.75	1.88	1.77
1972	2,300	1.50	1.49	1.42	1.50	1.45	1.50	1.59	1.51
1973	2,600	1.28	1.30	1.26	1.29	1.26	1.29	1.37	1.31
1974	3,100	1.00	1.00	1.00	1.00	1.00	1.00	1.00	1.00
1975	3,300	1.00	1.00	1.00	1.00	1.00	1.00	1.00	1.00

Source: *Udruzeni Rad i Osnovna Prava*, p. 52.

TABLE 9

DIFFERENCES IN RETIREMENT PENSIONS, BY REPUBLIC, ASSUMING
WAGES AND COEFFICIENTS IN TABLE 8, 1975

Republic	Amount of Pension (dinars)
Kosovo	3,189
Vojvodina	3,146
Bosnia and Hercegovina	3,094
Macedonia	3,056
Montenegro	3,003
Croatia	3,022
Serbia	3,020
Slovenia	2,986

SOURCE: *Udruzeni Rad i Osnovna Prava*, p. 53.

wage fund and other internal funds, including the business fund. Allocations to the business fund add to the organization's capital stock, decreasing the short-run level of the wage fund. A worker who retires and leaves the organization would not receive the future increments resulting from the capital investments that his previous sacrifices made possible. This restriction could result in a shortened time horizon for workers, a higher discount rate than would have prevailed, and a bias against self-financed investments. To grant workers who leave the organization a right to future returns from its earnings would be a step toward the creation of private property rights in capital goods. The Yugoslav government is clearly not ready for such a step.

The 1974 Constitution states that dohodak belongs only to those who combine current labor with the means of production. However, the law says that retirees have the right to participate in the economic growth of their respective regions. The government maintains that annual increments in current workers' real incomes reflect the returns on previously made investments. Thus, retirees and their families should participate in that growth of real income which they helped to finance.

In Serbia the annual adjustment in retirement benefits must be at least one-third of the rate of growth of real incomes. Since a worker's income is a combination of his wage and returns from capital, the adjustment (imperfect as it may be) is supposed to reflect the marginal contribution of capital to the worker's increment in total income. For example, retirement benefits were increased by 2.3 percent in 1975 over and above the adjustment for inflation.

Periodic Adjustments. Periodic adjustments attempt to provide a measure of equality among those who retired some time ago and more recent retirees and their families. For example, in 1974 all retirement benefits granted before December 1964 were increased by 6.4 percent while retirement benefits granted between January 1965 and June 1966 were increased by 6.2 percent.

Financing Retirement and Disability Benefits

Each regional social security system makes its own projection of expected expenditures and financial needs for the coming year. The community's need for tax revenues from workers is also affected by the level of current reserves. If reserves have fallen, tax collections may need to exceed expected expenditures, and vice versa. Tax rates differ from one republic to another and from one year to another. Yugoslavia has a pay-as-you-go social security system, as in the United States.

The most important source of revenue for financing retirement and disability benefits is a proportional tax on the wage fund, although a part of the member organization tax liability is paid from dohodak. There is no upper ceiling on taxable earnings as there is in the United States, nor is there any earned income credit for the personal income tax.[1] In addition, only contracted earnings are taxed: monetary rewards, prizes, and the like are not subject to the retirement and disability tax. Tax rates depend on the number of beneficiaries, relative levels of retirement and disability benefits, personal incomes, and other factors in each region.

The second source of revenue for financing retirement and disability programs is an additional tax paid by employees who receive more than one year's credit for each year of service—for instance, coal miners who receive one and one-half years of credit for each year of service. They have to pay an additional tax in proportion to the credit they receive.

Another tax used to finance disability benefits is paid by self-managing organizations, communities, and private firms that are responsible for disability claims in excess of the average for their region. This tax varies from one industry to another, depending on

---

[1] Because of the earned income credit, in the United States low-income persons with children are, in effect, relieved of paying payroll taxes for social security.

TABLE 10

Retirement, Survivors', and Disability Tax Rates, 1965–1977

Year	Yugoslavia[a]	Bosnia and Hercegovina	Montenegro	Croatia	Macedonia	Slovenia	Serbia	Kosovo	Vojvodina
1965	10.40	9.10	9.20	11.20	6.90	11.60	10.20	N.A.	N.A.
1966	10.22	8.95	9.92	10.60	6.25	11.40	10.50	N.A.	N.A.
1967	11.17	10.40	11.62	12.20	7.90	12.20	10.70	N.A.	N.A.
1968	11.22	10.25	10.50	12.40	8.30	12.50	10.65	N.A.	N.A.
1969	12.21	10.25	10.50	14.50	8.30	12.70	11.65	N.A.	N.A.
1970	12.21	10.25	10.50	14.50	8.30	12.70	11.65	9.78	12.55
1971	12.21	10.25	10.50	14.50	8.50	12.70	11.65	9.78	12.55
1972	12.21	10.25	10.50	14.50	8.50	12.70	11.65	9.78	12.55
1973	12.21	10.25	10.50	14.50	8.50	12.70	11.65	9.78	12.55
1974	N.A.	N.A.	10.50	N.A.	N.A.	N.A.	13.00	N.A.	N.A.
1975	N.A.	N.A.	11.40	N.A.	N.A.	N.A.	13.00	N.A.	N.A.
1976	N.A.	N.A.	12.30	N.A.	N.A.	N.A.	13.00	N.A.	N.A.
1977	N.A.	N.A.	12.30	N.A.	N.A.	N.A.	13.00	N.A.	N.A.

N.A.: Not available.

[a] Weighted average.

Source: I. Salihagic, *Razvoj Potrosnje u Penzijskom i Invalidskom Osiguranju u Yugoslaviji* (Zagreb, 1975), p. 425. Data for Serbia (1974–1977) were obtained privately by the author.

its "experience rating." This is expected to induce self-managing organizations to invest in safety equipment. For example, coal miners in Serbia pay an additional tax of 0.3 percent while construction workers pay an additional tax of 0.1 percent.

Table 10 shows the wide variation in social security tax rates among republics and autonomous provinces, from 8.5 percent in Macedonia in 1973 to 14.5 percent in Croatia. Except for Serbia and Montenegro, I could not find data for the other republics after 1973. Because the system of calculating these taxes varies, it is not clear whether additional taxes are always included.

4
Health Benefits

The production and distribution of health services in Yugoslavia are fully socialized. Physicians and dentists cannot sell their services in open markets, almost all Yugoslavs receive health services through regional self-managing communities of interest, and health programs are financed by proportional taxes on the incomes of the insured. Since medical care in Yugoslavia is "free," individuals have incentives to overconsume medical services, those providing services have incentives to shirk, and the government faces high monitoring costs. Socialized medicine generally fails to result in cost-minimizing behavior. Yet the Yugoslav variant of socialized medicine is an interesting and original attempt to develop organizational forms that generate incentives for the participants to minimize cost.

The role of the Yugoslav government in the production and distribution of medical services is only a supervisory one. The government modifies and changes the rules, monitors self-management agreements, and enforces their conformity with the law. The government's objective is to bring together the insured and the insurers, and to encourage them to participate actively in the production and distribution of health services. Self-management agreements are intended to strengthen the insured's perception of a link between his tax payments on the one hand and health benefits that he receives on the other.

The law mandates that those insured for health services include virtually all citizens. In effect, it is difficult to identify a group of citizens in Yugoslavia that is not eligible to receive medical care.

Types of Benefits

Health benefits in Yugoslavia can be classified into four groups: obligatory protection of health, contractual protection of health, compensation for lost income, and travel expenses. The last two benefits are not covered in many social security programs in other countries. These benefits are provided by the regional health organization and are available to the insured from the first day of accident or illness.

Obligatory Protection. Obligatory protection of health defines medical care that must be provided for all citizens. It includes prevention and treatment of tuberculosis; prevention and treatment of all contagious diseases; immunizations against various diseases; treatment of mental disorders; all medical services associated with pregnancy; birth control pills; complete health protection for children below age fifteen; complete health protection for all children regularly attending secondary schools, technical schools, and institutions of higher learning until the end of schooling or twenty-six years of age, whichever occurs first; prevention and treatment of diabetes; health education; and complete health protection for all citizens over sixty-five.

Contractual Protection. The regional health organizations must provide additional health benefits over and above the obligatory protection of health. The self-managing community of interest for health of Kraljevo in Serbia, for example, provides, among others, the following health benefits over and above the obligatory medical care: medical examination by a physician of the insured's choice, hospital care, laboratory tests, all dental work, and prescribed drugs. There are only small differences from one region to another.

Compensation for Loss of Income. The insured is eligible to be compensated for loss of income whenever he is temporarily unable to work because of illness or injury, when he is undergoing medical examinations, when he is quarantined, when he is taking care of another member of the family, and when he is assigned to take an ill or injured person to a medical institution in another city. In addition, a pregnant woman is entitled to compensation for loss of income during her absence from work, and so is the mother of a child up to three years old who is ill.

The insured is entitled to receive compensation for loss of income from the very first day of his absence from work. However, the insured's work organization usually bears the cost of compensation during the first thirty days. After that initial period, the cost is borne by the self-managing community of interest. Having the insured's work organization rather than the self-managing community of interest bear the cost for the first thirty days does provide some pressure on persons to reduce sick leave. This is one way in which the system of health insurance in Yugoslavia has been modified to encourage cost reduction. In some regions the self-managing community of interest compensates the insured for loss of income from the first day of his absence from work. On this point, some differences exist between individual republics. For example, in Serbia self-managing communities of interest are immediately responsible for the loss of income because of pregnancy, care of a sick infant, and accompanying a sick or injured person to another city. In Slovenia this responsibility is extended to include quarantined persons.

Compensation for the insured's loss of income is based on his monthly earnings in the year preceding the one in which he became eligible for compensation. The programs in various regions show some slight differences in the amount of compensation the insured is entitled to, with the amount depending on the length of the illness, the number of dependents, and other factors. In the Kraljevo region of Serbia, for example, the insured receives 85 percent of his income base during the first thirty days of absence from work, and 100 percent of his income afterwards (or a fraction thereof if he is only partially unable to work). If the insured is single he receives only 50 percent of his income, if he has one dependent he gets 90 percent of his income, and if he has two dependents he receives 100 percent of his income. When the absence from work is caused by injuries or illness contracted at work, the insured always gets 100 percent of his income. The insured's compensation for loss of income is adjusted for annual increments in his earnings (when the absence from work exceeds one year).

Travel Expenses. The insured is entitled to be reimbursed for the cost of travel, including hotel, food, and other incidental expenses, when his physician or clinic sends him to another city for medical examination or medical treatment, or when he has to travel (as is often the case in some remote parts of the country) in order to see a physician. In the Kraljevo region the self-management agreement states that the insured is entitled to round-trip bus or train fare (tourist class), per diem allowance of 50–120 dinars ($3–7), and an escort (who receives the same travel allowance plus compensation for loss of income).

Fees

Health services are paid for mainly through a proportional tax on incomes. However, the insured pays for some health services—in the

Kraljevo region, for example, the insured pays a flat fee of 5 dinars (28 cents) for each prescribed drug, and 30 percent of hospital costs during the period of his recuperation from an illness or injury not caused at work. Although the use of fees appears to conflict with the goals of socialized medicine, it provides incentives for persons to economize on the use of hospital care and drugs.

Financing Health Programs

The regional self-managing communities of interest for health make annual projections of the cost of health programs in their respective areas. The laws enacted by individual republics require the financing of health programs. The principal sources of funds are a tax on personal income, an additional tax, and a special tax. Given the projected expenditures on the one hand and the sources of funds on the other, regional self-managing communities of interest impose tax rates that are expected to raise the required amount of revenues.

The most important source of funds for financing health programs is a proportional tax on personal incomes. This tax is levied on the incomes of all working people in self-managing organizations and communities, on retirement and disability benefits, on the total income of farmers from agricultural and other activities, on the contractual income of employees in the private sector, on the total earnings of owners of small businesses, on the stipends of students, and on an amount equal to the legal minimum wage in their respective republics for those who participate in public work of social significance.

An additional tax is levied on the wage fund of self-managing organizations and private employers whose medical claims exceed the average for their (or similar) industries. A special tax may be imposed by a regional self-managing community of interest if its regular revenues turn out to be inadequate to cover actual expenditures. This tax is paid on the wage fund of all organizations in the region. Finally, if a regional self-managing community of interest cannot cover the cost of obligatory health programs, the appropriate republic is supposed to provide the additional revenue needed.

As Table 11 shows, the average tax rates for health in the republics and autonomous provinces vary from one republic to another. Although the average health tax rate in Yugoslavia was 8.66 percent in 1976, the average rates in the republics and autonomous provinces varied from 7.05 percent in Montenegro to 10.31 percent in Slovenia.

Tax rates for financing health programs also vary from one

TABLE 11

Average Health Tax Rates in the Republics and Autonomous Provinces in Yugoslavia, 1965–1976

Year	Yugo-slavia	Bosnia and Herce-govina	Monte-negro	Croatia	Mace-donia	Slovenia	Serbia	Kosovo	Vojvo-dina
1965	8.38	8.60	8.00	8.40	8.30	8.30	8.70	N.A.	N.A.
1966	7.55	7.60	7.50	7.80	8.00	7.00	7.40	N.A.	N.A.
1967	5.44	6.00	5.30	5.20	5.60	5.00	5.60	N.A.	N.A.
1968	5.40	6.00	5.20	5.20	5.60	5.00	5.40	N.A.	N.A.
1969	5.57	6.00	5.20	5.70	5.60	5.20	5.70	N.A.	N.A.
1970	5.57	6.00	5.20	5.70	5.60	5.20	5.72	N.A.	N.A.
1971	8.11	7.68	6.97	8.88	7.71	10.81	7.63	7.60	7.57
1972	8.11	7.68	6.97	8.88	7.71	10.81	7.63	7.60	7.57
1973	8.00	8.05	6.94	8.33	7.65	9.67	8.04	7.60	7.65
1974	8.73	8.10	7.12	8.98	7.78	10.98	10.05	7.60	9.25
1975	8.77	8.96	7.18	9.31	7.83	10.58	9.04	8.39	8.85
1976	8.66	8.13	7.05	9.69	7.68	10.31	9.11	9.10	8.18

N.A.: Not available.

Source: Privately obtained by the author. This table includes additional and special taxes.

region to another within the same republic. For example, the regional self-managing community of interest of Kraljevo established a proportional health tax of 8.65 percent for 1977 (exclusive of additional and special taxes). Further, the self-managing community of interest instructed its administrative agency (sluzba) to allocate the revenue collected as follows: 30 percent for financing obligatory health programs, 5.15 percent for financing the additional health programs provided, and 0.5 percent for financing injuries and illness contracted at work. In addition, the self-managing community of interest of Kraljevo established flat monthly fees of 130 dinars (approximately $7) for unemployed workers (paid by the employment agency), 120 dinars for priests, 60 dinars for volunteers at public works, and 120 dinars for students not receiving stipends.

5

The Number of Beneficiaries and the Aggregate Cost of Social Security

Statistical data on the social security system in Yugoslavia are available on the number of people receiving retirement and disability benefits, expenditures for social security programs in dinars and as a percentage of GNP, the breakdown of expenditures for social security programs by republics for 1976, and the average daily absence from work for reasons covered by health programs. These data from 1967 to 1976 are shown in Tables 12 to 17.

Yugoslav gross national product (called social product) leaves out as "nonproductive services," activities such as state administration, personal services, and cultural activities. Thus, the concept is not directly comparable with the gross national product in the United States. Also, individual republics do not always use the same methods in calculating their statistical data. The social security programs differ from one republic to another and so does the number of people who are eligible to receive social security benefits. For these reasons, it would be misleading to try to compare the costs and benefits of social security programs in Yugoslavia and in the United States.

The cost of social security programs in Yugoslavia is relatively high, amounting to about 13 percent of GNP in 1977. In terms of its growth rate, the cost is even more apparent. From 1967 to 1977, Yugoslavia's GNP in current prices grew rapidly—at an average annual rate of 21.43 percent. During the same period, total money expenditure for social security programs rose even more rapidly—at a rate of 24.14 percent. Expenditures for retirement and disability programs increased at a rate of 24.29 percent, while expenditures for health programs grew by 23.94 percent.

In real terms, the Yugoslav GNP in the 1967–1977 period grew at an annual rate of 5.79 percent, while total social security expendi-

TABLE 12

Number of People Receiving Retirement, Survivors', and Disability Benefits in Yugoslavia, 1967–1976

Year	Retirees		Survivors' Benefits		Disability Benefits		Others	
	Number (thousands)	Percentage of labor force	Number (thousands)	Percentage of labor force	Number (thousands)	Percentage of labor force	Number (thousands)	Percentage of labor force
1967	375	10	245	7	374	10	129	4
1968	391	11	258	7	401	11	130	4
1969	409	11	272	7	412	11	143	4
1970	430	11	287	7	419	11	145	4
1971	450	11	303	7	424	10	143	3
1972	477	11	319	7	431	10	147	3
1973	467	11	330	8	436	10	150	3
1974	486	11	348	8	448	10	153	3
1975	499	10	365	8	454	9	160	3
1976	508	10	378	8	467	9	172	3

Source: *Statisticki Godisnjak Jugoslavije, 1977*, pp. 115 and 317.

tures rose at a rate of 8.38 percent. Expenditures for health programs rose 8.20 percent a year, and expenditures for retirement and disability programs rose 8.50 percent a year. The rate of growth in total real expenditures for social security programs exceeded the real GNP growth rate by an average of 2.59 percent a year and in money terms by 2.71 percent annually.

Table 12 shows that the ratio of retirees to the labor force did not increase in Yugoslavia from 1967 to 1976, while the ratio of disabled workers actually fell. The rate of growth of expenditures for retirement and disability benefits in excess of the GNP growth rate must be due to either an increase in the average number of years of service of recent retirees or a higher rate of increase in benefits relative to workers' incomes. In fact, I was repeatedly told during my visit in Yugoslavia (summer of 1978) that thanks to automatic adjustments for inflation and real growth, social security retirement benefits are the best hedge against inflation in Yugoslavia.

The administrative costs of social security programs in Yugoslavia, as shown in Table 17, do not appear to be excessive. However, the fact that administrative costs have remained relatively stable as a percentage of social security expenditures means that the budgets of sluzba have increased at a higher rate than the Yugoslav GNP.

TABLE 13

NUMBER OF PEOPLE RECEIVING RETIREMENT, SURVIVORS', AND DISABILITY
BENEFITS BY REPUBLICS AND AUTONOMOUS PROVINCES, 1976

	Retirees		Survivors' Benefits		Disability Benefits	
Republic	Number (thousands)	Percentage of labor force	Number (thousands)	Percentage of labor force	Number (thousands)	Percentage of labor force
Bosnia and Hercegovina	51	7	59	8	66	9
Montenegro	13	12	10	9	15	14
Croatia	143	12	104	9	146	12
Macedonia	31	9	18	5	18	5
Slovenia	97	14	55	8	51	7
Serbia	113	9	79	6	99	8
Kosovo	6	4	10	7	17	12
Vojvodina	53	11	42	8	54	11

SOURCE: *Statisticki Godisnjak Jugoslavije*, 1977, pp. 387 and 526.

TABLE 14

TOTAL EXPENDITURES FOR HEALTH PROGRAMS AND RETIREMENT, SURVIVORS', AND DISABILITY BENEFITS IN YUGOSLAVIA, 1967–1977

Year	Retirement, Survivors', and Disability Benefits		Health Programs		Health, Retirement, Survivors', and Disability Programs	
	Total expenditures (millions of dinars)	Percentage of GNP	Total expenditures (millions of dinars)	Percentage of GNP	Total expenditures (millions of dinars)	Percentage of GNP
1967	6,106	5.88	4,416	4.26	10,522	10.14
1968	7,109	6.35	4,736	4.23	11,845	10.58
1969	8,587	6.51	5,743	4.35	14,320	10.85
1970	10,935	6.95	7,311	4.65	18,246	11.61
1971	13,851	6.77	9,232	4.51	23,083	11.29
1972	18,243	7.43	11,751	4.79	29,997	12.22
1973	21,152	6.90	14,353	4.69	35,505	11.59
1974	27,452	6.74	19,325	4.74	46,777	11.49
1975	35,469	7.05	25,627	5.09	61,096	12.15
1976	45,072	7.56	33,324	5.59	78,396	13.16
1977	53,714	7.42	37,780	5.23	91,494	12.66

SOURCE: *Statisticki Godisnjak Jugoslavije, 1977*, pp. 144, 316, and 317.

TABLE 15

TOTAL EXPENDITURES FOR HEALTH PROGRAMS AND RETIREMENT, SURVIVORS', AND DISABILITY BENEFITS BY REPUBLICS AND AUTONOMOUS PROVINCES, 1976

Republic	Retirement, Survivors', and Disability Benefits		Health Programs	
	Total expenditures (millions of dinars)	Percentage of republic's GNP	Total expenditures (millions of dinars)	Percentage of republic's GNP
Bosnia and Hercegovina	5,393	7.34	3,739	4.83
Montenegro	1,237	12.17	647	6.36
Croatia	13,181	8.45	10,481	6.72
Macedonia	1,802	5.53	1,562	4.79
Slovenia	7,587	7.43	4,930	4.83
Serbia	10,044	6.93	8,141	5.62
Kosovo	1,010	8.81	908	7.92
Vojvodina	4,818	7.36	2,916	4.45

SOURCE: *Statisticki Godisnjak Jugoslavije,* 1977, pp. 406, 525, and 526.

TABLE 16

Average Daily Absence from Work for Reasons Covered by Health Programs, 1976

Republic	Daily Absence	Percentage of Republic's Labor Force
Bosnia and Hercegovina	34,594	5
Montenegro	3,683	3
Croatia	71,480	6
Macedonia	7,600	2
Slovenia	35,543	5
Serbia	59,625	5
Kosovo	2,863	2
Vojvodina	22,018	4

Source: *Statisticki Godisnjak Jugoslavije,* 1977, pp. 387 and 525.

TABLE 17

ADMINISTRATIVE COSTS (SLUZBA) OF SOCIAL SECURITY PROGRAMS, 1976

Republic	Administration of Health Programs (millions of dinars)	Percentage of Total Expenditures	Administration of Retirement and Disability Programs (millions of dinars)	Percentage of Total Expenditures
Bosnia and Hercegovina	109	3	139	3
Montenegro	22	3	39	3
Croatia	222	2	261	2
Macedonia	44	3	42	2
Slovenia	109	2	98	1
Serbia	165	2	238	2
Kosovo	32	3	35	3
Vojvodina	93	3	105	2

SOURCE: *Statisticki Godisnjak Jugoslavije, 1977*, pp. 525–26.

6
Summary

Social security programs in Yugoslavia have broad coverage, offer substantial benefits, and impose a heavy and growing burden on the national economy. In those respects, the differences between social security systems in Yugoslavia and most other countries, including the United States, are primarily quantitative. Comparative studies on the differences in social security costs and benefits should certainly be useful in providing a better perspective for the evaluation of our own social security programs. However, the importance of the Yugoslav social security system lies more in its qualitative differences from the one in the United States.

The Yugoslav social security system differs from those in most other countries in its organizational structure, its method of financing, and its degree of decentralization. Not only are those key features of the system original in their concept, but their implementation is bound to have allocative implications that deserve further study. The Yugoslav social security system, as it matures, may suggest ways in which incentives that generate less wasteful behavior can be injected into systems of intergenerational transfer payments.

The organizational structure of the Yugoslav social security system tends to have two major effects. The first—an institutional one —is a de-bureaucratization of the system. The number of people actually employed to administer social security programs in various regions of the country may not be fewer than in a centralized system, but the regional administrative units (sluzba) are largely independent of one another, subject to greater local controls, and therefore more controllable.

The second effect of the Yugoslav social security system—a behavioral one—is on the system of incentives. The organizational